Electricity

Jacqueline Dineen

Watts Books
London • New York • Sydney

© 1995 Watts Books

Watts Books
96 Leonard Street
London EC2A 4RH

Franklin Watts Australia
14 Mars Road
Lane Cove
NSW 2060

UK ISBN: 0 7496 1446 3

10 9 8 7 6 5 4 3 2 1

Editor: Claire Llewellyn
Design: Caroline Ginesi
Artwork: Jamie Medlin
          Mainline Design
Cover artwork: Hugh Dixon
Picture Research: Brooks Krikler Research
                  Juliet Duff

A CIP catalogue record for this book is
available from the British Library

Dewey Decimal Classification: 333.79

Printed in Italy by G. Canale and C. SpA

Contents

What is electricity?

Electricity, heat and light are all types of **energy**. All living things need energy. It can be stored and released to do useful work. In a power station, burning **fuel** releases energy to make electricity. Energy can move from one place to another. When you turn on a light, electricity flows to the bulb. The energy is changed into heat and light.

▽ Electricity gives us heat and light. Can you imagine a city at night without electricity?

Static electricity

Static electricity is all around us. It is caused by **friction**, when two surfaces rub together. When you pull a jumper over your head, you sometimes hear a crackling sound. This is static electricity. The word 'static' means 'staying still'. Static electricity does not flow along wires.

▽Static electricity generated by a Van de Graaff machine produces sparks between two nails.

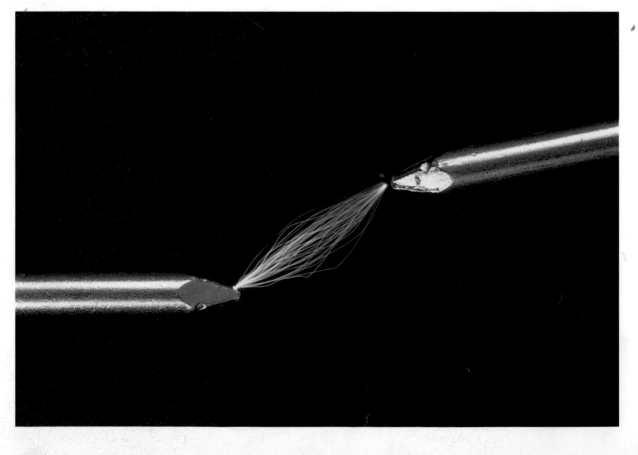

▷ Rub a balloon hard against your jumper, and then stick it on the wall. It will stay there until the electric charge weakens.

▽ If you comb your hair hard, there is friction between your hair and the comb.

Electricity in nature

Lightning is a huge flash of electricity. It lights up the sky during a thunderstorm. Lightning is caused by **electric charges** building up in storm clouds. The charges are attracted to opposite charges in the same cloud, in other clouds or on the ground. They jump across the sky as a huge electric spark. It is so powerful that it can kill people if it strikes them.

▷ We see the energy from the electric charge as a huge flash of light zigzagging across the sky.

▽ Some sea creatures have built-in electricity. They use it to detect other animals, protect themselves, and stun their prey.

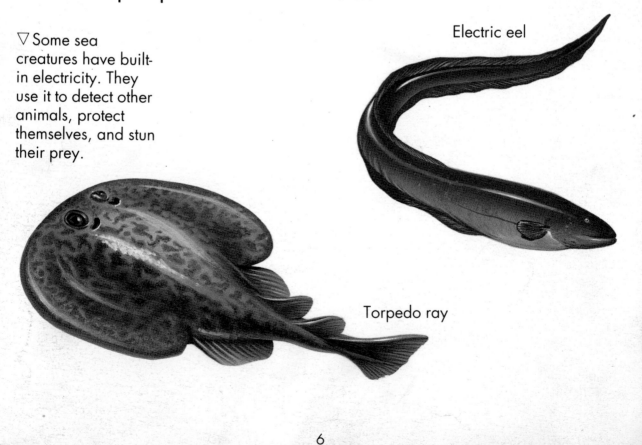

Electric eel

Torpedo ray

6

Discovering electricity

The ancient Greeks discovered electricity more than 2000 years ago. They found that if a piece of amber was rubbed against a cloth such as silk, then dust, straw and feathers all stuck to the amber. The word electricity comes from the Greek word 'elektron' which means amber. In 1752, an American called Benjamin Franklin proved that thunderclouds contain electricity.

▷ Electricity always takes the easiest path to the ground. Lightning passes safely down the metal conductor, and avoids striking the building.

▷ The Greeks made jewellery from amber. They noticed that it attracted small things like feathers when it was rubbed against cloth.

▷ Benjamin Franklin tied a key to a kite string and flew it in a storm. Lightning struck the kite and travelled down to the key where it caused a spark. This dangerous experiment gave Franklin the idea for the lightning conductor.

What is a battery?

Electricity is not very useful until it is made to move. It will flow along wires to where it is needed. Electricity moving through wires is called an **electric current**. A battery can produce its own electricity. It was invented by an Italian scientist called Alessandro Volta, in about 1800.

▷ The first batteries were cumbersome. The electric current was produced by separating two different metals with paper soaked in salt water.

▷ Batteries are small, safe and can be carried from place to place. They come in different shapes and sizes and are used in toys, games and radios.

▽ Some batteries can be charged up by using a special charger. It is plugged into the electricity supply for a few hours.

Electric circuits

A battery gives electricity a boost of energy to get it moving. Electricity will not flow through everything. The substances it flows through, such as metal, are called **conductors**. The substances it cannot flow through, such as plastic and rubber, are known as **insulators**. If metal wires are connected to two points on the battery, they make a continuous pathway for the electricity. This is called a **circuit**.

▽ Inside a piece of flex are the metal wires which carry the electricity. The plastic coating stops the electricity leaking out.

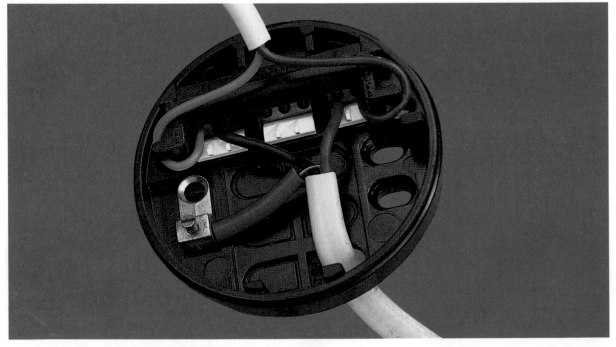

Making an electric circuit

Safety note: Always use batteries for these experiments. Never use an electric socket.

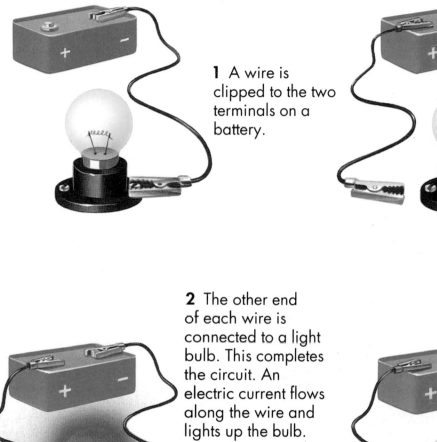

1 A wire is clipped to the two terminals on a battery.

2 The other end of each wire is connected to a light bulb. This completes the circuit. An electric current flows along the wire and lights up the bulb.

3 If the circuit is broken, the current stops flowing. The light goes out.

Producing electricity

Think about the 101 ways we use electricity each day. This wouldn't be possible without a continuous and very powerful flow of electricity. The electricity for our daily needs is produced in power stations, using a method discovered by a British scientist, Michael Faraday, in 1831. He produced an electric current using wire and a magnet.

▷ When Faraday moved a magnet in and out of a coil of wire, an electric current flowed through the wire.

Inside a power station

When Michael Faraday moved a magnet in and out of a coil of wire, he used energy from his own body. In power stations, a **generator** is used to produce a continuous supply of electricity. It has an enormous magnet surrounded by a coil of copper wire. As the magnet spins, a powerful electric current is produced in the wire.

▽ The electricity we use each day is produced in huge power stations.

Generating electricity

The magnet in the generator turns to produce electricity.

copper wire

magnet

shaft

Inside the generator is a wheel with blades, called a turbine. A shaft connected to the turbine drives the generator.

The magnet is fixed to the shaft. When the turbine spins, the magnet spins and produces a current in the wire.

Driving the generator

Many generators are driven by burning huge amounts of fuel to release energy. Coal, oil or gas is burned to boil water and make clouds of steam. The steam rushes through pipes and turns the blades of the **turbine**. A great deal of energy is used to produce a constant supply of steam and keep the turbine spinning.

▷ The turbine inside a generator is turned by steam. As it turns, a connecting shaft also turns a magnet, and produces an electric current.

▽ This diagram shows how coal that is burned in a power station will produce the energy to drive a generator.

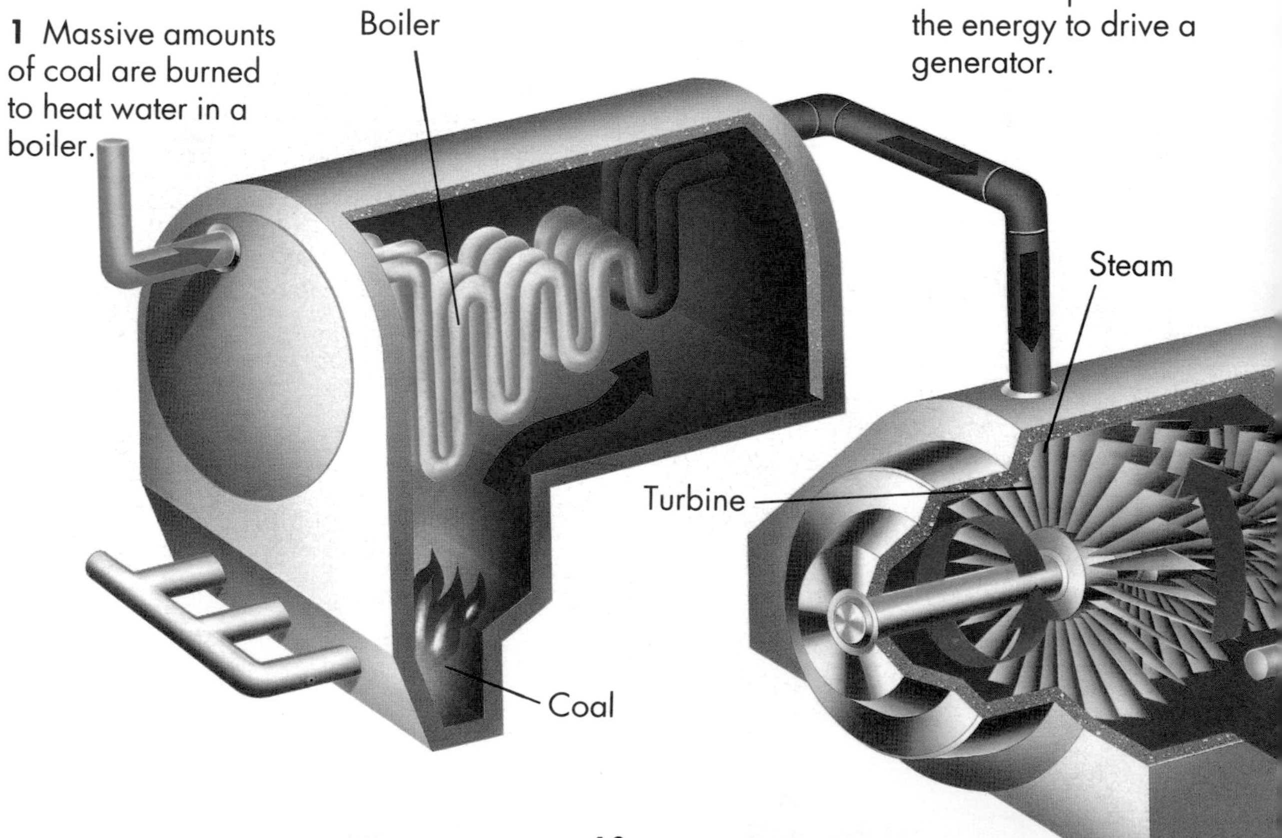

1 Massive amounts of coal are burned to heat water in a boiler.

Boiler

Coal

Steam

Turbine

2 Powerful jets of steam strike the blades of the turbine and make it spin.

Electricity to you

Thick wires called cables carry the electricity from the power station to everyone who needs it. In open countryside, the cables are held up by metal towers called pylons, but in towns many of them are buried underground. These large cables are called the mains. The cables from power stations are all linked together to form a huge network or grid.

▽ The power station generates electricity which is carried through long cables to our homes, offices and factories. This kind of electricity cannot be stored.

Pylons hold the cables high above people and buildings. A constant supply of electricity flows through the wires.

Power station

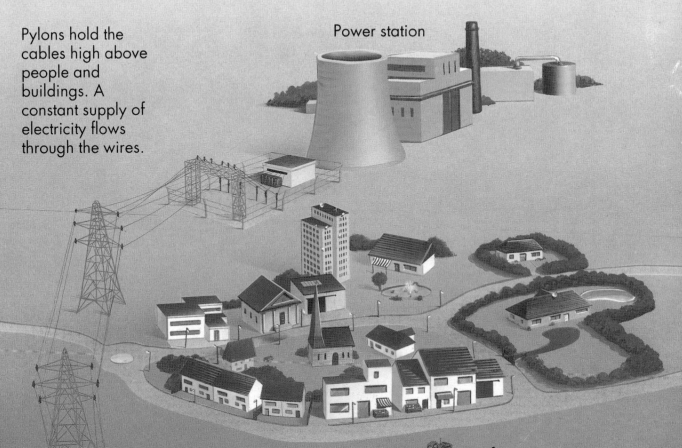

If a power station cannot provide enough electricity for its area, extra supplies can be sent from another part of the grid.

Electric light and heat

The electric light bulb was invented by an American, Thomas Edison, in 1879. Inside every glass bulb, you will see a thin wire called a **filament**. A flow of electricity heats up the filament until it is so hot that it glows and gives out a bright light. Electric fires, kettles, irons and toasters also work by heating up metal.

▽ Modern light bulbs are filled with a mixture of harmless gases to stop the filament burning.

▷ One of the first electric light bulbs. Edison found that the filament would burn if it was exposed to the air. So he enclosed it in a sealed bulb which contained no air at all.

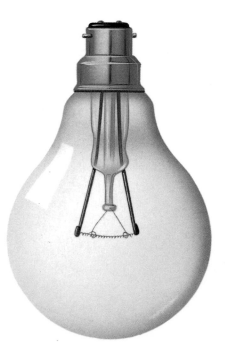

▷ Inside an electric kettle is a metal part called the element. This becomes so hot that it boils the water in the kettle. It is the element inside them that heats up a toaster and an iron.

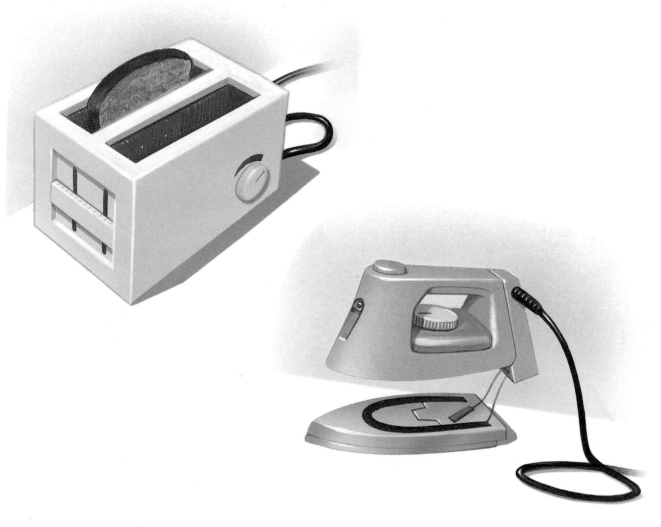

Electricity in the home

Electricity provides heat and light in the home and it also makes machines work. In the kitchen, there may be a cooker, washing machine, dishwasher, and food mixer. In the sitting room there will probably be a television, a video recorder, and a CD player. Many homes also have a telephone, a computer, and household machines such as a hoover.

▷ It's hard to imagine a kitchen without electricity. Electric machines help us do our work quickly and easily.

▽ Electricity is an important part of our lives. Many machines work at the flick of a switch.

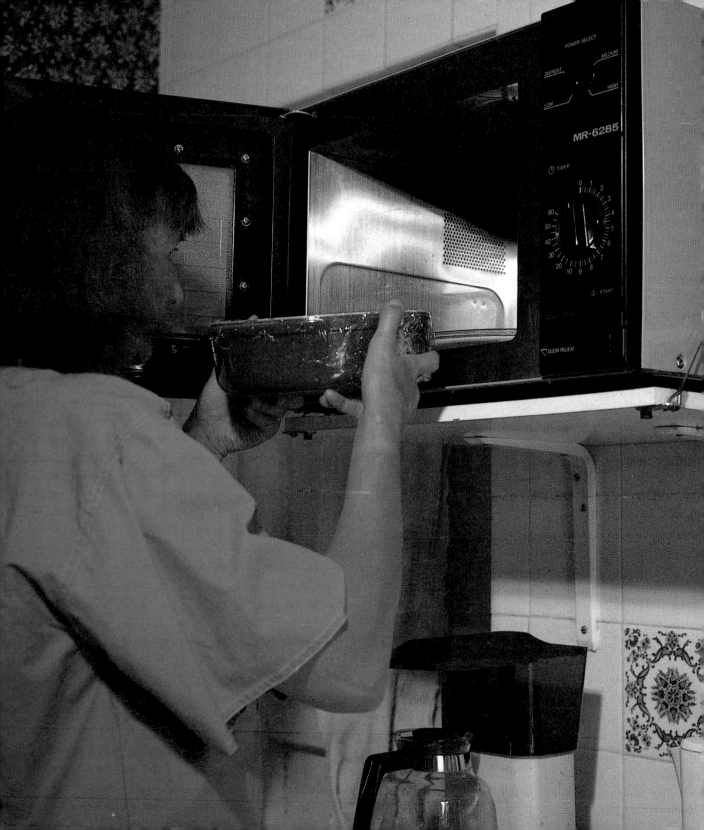

Electricity at work

Factories rely on electricity to work their machines. Electricity powers the computers, typewriters and telephones which are all used in offices. The life-saving machinery in hospitals runs on electricity. Shops use electricity to keep food cold and fresh, and to work lifts, escalators, automatic doors, and the computers at check-outs.

▷ Electric trains are powered by overhead cables. Commuters depend on them to get them to work.

▷ Electrocardiograph machines help doctors find out what is wrong with their patients.

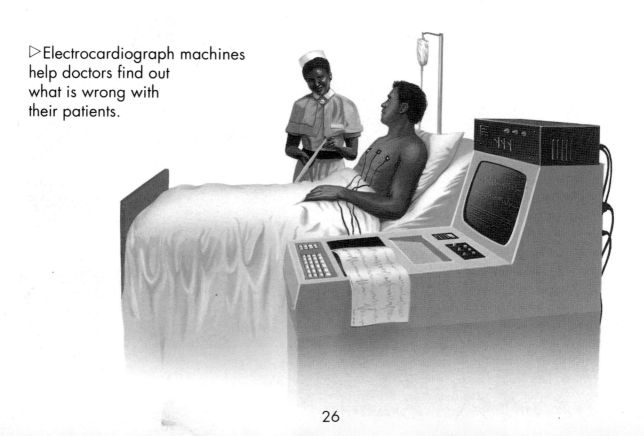

▷ Most modern
offices depend more
and more on
computers,
photocopiers and
fax machines. They
all run on electricity.

Use it safely

We all use electricity every day without giving it a thought. Yet electricity is very dangerous, and can kill if it is not used properly. Always remember the safety rules. Never play or experiment with switches or sockets. Never touch a switch or socket with wet hands. Electricity and water are extremely dangerous.

▽ Faulty wiring can cause fires. Old wiring should always be replaced by a qualified electrician.

▽ Never use cracked or broken plugs, or wiring that has frayed.

▽ Keep water and electricity apart. Never use water near an electric socket.

▷ Never run two appliances from one plug.

Things to do

- Imagine that you are living in the days before electricity was discovered. Draw a picture of you and your family with the things you would be using. How would you light the room? How would you cook?

- How many pieces of electrical equipment do you have at home? First, have a guess. Then, go into every room and count them all. Did you have more or less than you thought?

- Plan an all-electric dream house. Don't forget the garage and garden. Draw a plan of your house with a list of all the electrical things you would have in it.

Useful addresses:

Understanding Electricity Educational
  Service
The Electricity Association
30 Millbank
London SW1P 4RD

Information Officer
Corporate Communications
National Power plc
Windmill Hill Business Park
Whitehill Way
Swindon SN5 9NX

Glossary

amber Hardened sap from pine trees. It has an attractive orange colour and is often used to make jewellery.

circuit The complete circular path of an electric current.

conductor A substance that acts as a path for electricity.

electric current The flow of electricity.

element The heating part of a piece of electrical equipment.

energy The power which does work and drives machines.

filament The thin metal wire in a light bulb.

friction The rubbing of two surfaces against each other.

fuel A material like coal or wood that can be burned to provide heat or to make machinery work.

generator A machine for producing electricity.

grid The network of electricity cables which connects power stations, and allows electricity to be sent from one area to another.

insulator A substance that does not allow electricity to pass through it.

static electricity Electricity which does not flow.

turbine The part of a generator or any engine which is made to turn by the force of pressure.

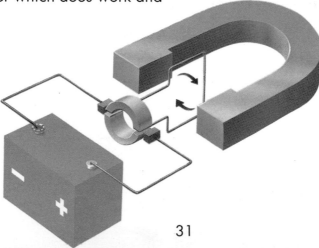

Index

Photographic credits:
Central Electricity Generating
Board 19; Chris Fairclough 12;
Robert Harding Picture Library 16;
The Hutchison Library © J. G. Fuller 9;
Spectrum Colour Library 28,
© A. R. Smith 20; Science Photo Library
© Adam Hart-Davis 4, © Kent Wood 7,
© Jerome Yeats 11, © Alax Bartel 15;
Solution Pictures 25; ZEFA 3, 27.